In the Light of the Full Moon

In the Light
of the Full Moon

Dispersions, Glimpses, and Reflections

Don Langford

Published by D S Langford Publishing
Columbus, OH 43229
https://dslangfordpublishing.com

Printed in the United States

Cover art: Don Langford, *Moon over Firehole Canyon*, 2022

Names: Langford, Don, author
Title: *In the Light of the Full Moon: Dispersions, Glimpses, and Reflections* / Don Langford

ISBN 979-8-9867546-0-4 (pbk.)

Library of Congress Control Number: 2022915695

A special thank you to Steve Abbott for his editorial observations, always helpful suggestions, and friendly support. Additional appreciation and thanks to friend and colleague, Jeremy Glazier, for his unwavering support and professional encouragement.

First paperback edition, 2022

For Marlene

Gaining enlightenment is like the moon reflecting in
        the water
The moon does not get wet, nor is the water disturbed.
Although its light is extensive and great, the moon is
        reflected even in a puddle an inch across.
The whole moon and the whole sky are reflected in a
        dew-drop in the grass, in one drop of water.
Enlightenment does not disturb the person, just as the
        moon does not disturb the water.

                    Eihei Dogen (1200-1253)
                    The Way of Everyday Life

When I look at the moon
My mind goes roaming
Till I live again
the Autumns that I knew long ago.

                    Saigyo (1118-1190)

I enjoy the simple path
between dark vines and mountain caves
the wilderness has room to roam
with white clouds for companions
there's a road but not to town
only mindless men can climb
at night I sit on the rocks alone
until the moon comes up Cold Mountain

                    Hanshan (1546-1623)
                    The Collected Songs of Cold Mountain

Contents

Part I: Dispersions

Part II: Glimpses

Part III: Reflections

About the Author

Acknowledgments

"Perseverance Furthers": *Gesture*
"On Visiting a Friend in the Camarillo Mental Institution": *Olentangy Review*
"Singing in the Key of Z": *The Lowell Review*
"Triptych": *Spring Street*
"Seismic Vertical": *petroglyph*
"In Amber": *Spring Street*
"Chuang Tzu and the Culture of Appropriate Suffering": *Kaleidoscope*
"Autumn": *Cornfield Review*
"Vivid Dreams, Antarctica" *Rhino*
"The Landlord Next Door": *The Fairfield Review*

Part I: Dispersions

The Landlord Next Door

Patching a crack in the walkway,
filling a small hole in his house
with cement, returning a cup of soil
to a hole left in the ground by squirrels,
the old man, my landlord, works
                              patiently.

The world's calamities can wait;
he harvests the tomatoes that he planted
from seed, waters the impatiens that grow
in fullest bright color by his porch,
turns the earth and worms in his garbage can of rich
                              dark soil.

He will disappear some days with his fishing pole
and box of floaters and sinkers, and a lunchbox;
he will disappear with the squirrel cage that he uses
to relocate squirrels to other wooded places,
perpetually moving each generation that moves into our
                              neighborhood.

He will disappear
and the world that never knew he was here
will be smaller because of his disappearance.
He will leave no big mark that he was here;
he tends to his lawn, removing the weeds
each spring and fall,
        the humblest of souls
        taking the littlest portions from this world
        and returning them back to the earth,
        working deliberately and slowly,
        keeping his little part of the world from falling apart.

The Monorail

There is no monorail conductor.
People enter the car to find others are already there.
Some get off, others get on, and the car moves along with precision.

There's no way to know where and when the ride originated.
A few people on the car remember someone
who had remembered someone else farther back along the rail
who speculated about a group of wise folks who
devoted their discourses to the importance of the monorail ride,
but they weren't especially concerned about where the ride started.

Others said they think they know where the ride began
and where it will end, even though we'll all have to depart
before the monorail reaches the end.

Some of the earlier travelers recorded a few of their ideas
and left them in the car,
others wrote books about what previous riders had said.

I've read a few of the books left in the car,
and occasionally I converse with other passengers to see
if they will offer any clues about where we've been
and where we're going.
A few people are saying that the destination is real
but the journey isn't.
Others say that all of the experience in the monorail is an illusion.

When I sit quietly it seems that there is nothing outside of the mind.

Seismic Vertical

— the point upon the earth's surface
vertically over the center of effort
or focal point, whence the earthquake's impulse proceeds,
or the vertical line connecting these two points—

Could we have known there were signs
in the motion of birds,
          the dog's ears,
            and the crickets' silence—
that beneath the calm surface of things
        our lives were trembling—
              breaking up—
                  rolling out of control?

Directly over the blind and silent fury
we lived our lives
as if these gentle contours of hill and valley
were something constant—
like unchanging friend, always there
to measure our shifting temperament,
        youthful folly,
            mid-life anxieties . . .

    always there to give the illusion
    that our disbelief in the solid
    unity and wholeness of things
    was itself an illusion.

For as long as these mountains and ravines
through which we have walked
these many years
remain still
amid the
seasonal
changes,

there would be for us
an ordered world
restrained by some logic to prevent it
from whirling into unexplained chaos.

But today, the winter trees might well have
sprouted wings and flown south
    like late arboreal geese;
the streams and pools that cooled us in summer
might just as well have boiled away
    into blue mist, leaving
     only a faint taste on our lips
        of ever having been here.
We did not read the signs;
there were no dung beetles to raise their antennae
to the charge of buffalo;
no noticeable formation of ice cracks
     in the standing water
     that would alert us to impending
        violent earth shake.

We were talking about the drives we once made
    along the winding California coastline,
ferns and foxglove in dew-laden summer mornings,
    along the steep ravines that dropped to the sea.
That's how blood vessels burst
     in one's brain
they say,—or in one's heart—
    waiting quietly, then exploding
      in the moment of calm,
as when you and I were caught in that green reminiscence,
     the quiet nostalgia
       of comfort in our own time,
not really thinking that this would last forever,
  but not believing that it could so suddenly roll over
  into something unimaginable,
    and vanish while we watched.

Singing in the Key of Z

We will celebrate these reverberations
        these deflections
                of light and surface
the ricocheting of what we mean—
    like glints
    and scraps that never
                congeal,
                coalesce.

    We will come to admire
the fractured places
            —the interstices—
                that look like pursed smiles
                        on the cobbled walkway,
or the line of a closed eye
pressing out the light;

kaleidoscopic color chips
rubbing their cubist
        edges
            running round,
                    cylindered
        and
                boxed in.

We grow content with the glaze,
                        the chips of colored glass, and
the way they float
        without history
                or meaning . . . over the scenery,
    cascading down from the overpasses,
    punched into smithereens
    like windshields crystallized . . .

                we are bedazzled
by the world turning to powder,

                        by our own
private minds, thinking
more alike,
entertained
                        beyond our wildest expectations—
thrilled numb
singing in our fashionable ennui
                before sleep.

The Pact

She said, "My name is fickleness,
my frown is longer than the day,
and you will not be able to ride
      the current
            far enough
to see where I conceal myself
from the world that you find
      so predictable
            and comforting."

I said, "I have lashed myself to the mast,
and I will swallow the sea
      before my next breath
and I will find you
      as I have done before
            and before."

She said, "We will find each other
      in our mutiny, count the breaths together,
only when you resurface
      in a world that was not meant for you,
           when you no longer know
            or remember
              that we once
          met when the waves washed us clean."

I said, "We will not recognize each other,
      so we must have a sign that takes us
        beyond the temporal;
        perhaps the frightful eyes, in drowning,
          will be our universal signature,
            our way of saying,
            'This is me
            if you care.'"

On Visiting a Friend in the
Camarillo Mental Institution

Is this what you wanted when you said,
"I am going to discover myself," and
began peeling away layer after layer from above
your high cheekbones,
pulling away the bones until the mirror
reflected only light?

Is this what you wanted when you said
there would be no more suffering,
no more to look for; no more looker?
Would clear white light have ever been enough for you?
They tell me you cannot hear your own howls at night—that you
have created a new language of wind and thunder;
that you have an eerie moan like someone who
has lost his way home—like someone who has too closely
seen the horrors of being human;
like someone imprisoned forever.

The nurse has said that you are trapped
inside a bag of skin, and that
it is too bad that I can't take you over to the window
and push you through the bars and release you
from this torment.

But, for another hour you and I sit together
in the filtered light.
I console myself with the thought that maybe
the blank stare on your face is really
supreme patience;
that you have already vacated this empty shell; that
we are merely propping pillows against the husk of a free spirit,
and that you, my dear friend, have left us
to make our own discoveries.

Yearning to Live Again

When he pronounced the words, "More death,"
we remembered the bardo
and Kelly thought it was Brigitte
and said so

so some of us laughed
while others frowned and said,
"Show your respect"
and you said, "For death,
          or for life's beauty?"

But that was thirty years ago
          when all of us were still alive

Now we know that laughing
is for the living;
the dead no longer laugh with us

          memory lives but for an instant
          among the living

and if we remember death
          and those who once lived among us,
                    it is because we, too,
          desire to be alive once again
          when laughter is free and accepted.

"Live more," was your refrain,
          your answer to those words
          on the other side of the bardo
          that made death seem
          more important than life.

"Live more," you said again,
          for emphasis.

11

Childplay and Coneflower

Today I thought how remarkable was that world
which dreamed itself into being
by that child who was me long ago.

When I was born the world was born,
then I learned that it had been here before me
but that was something I learned, not anything that I
could touch or smell, hold in my hands
like this coneflower root that I chewed on this morning.

The primordial mud was not something billions of years ago
to that child who sat in mud puddles watching the ooze
squeeze through clenched fists in the rain
or reaching down into the pond, scooping up the muck
and instantly feeling something magical and mysterious
before being taught to stop doing that.

I am returning to that world where the directness of it
is what shapes the connections to ancestral old brain experience.
What wonders there are in a clod of earth,
biting into a ripe tomato, juice running down the chin.
Even the bitter taste of this coneflower root reminds me
        of the sweet past, eating clover blossoms
        biting into grassy shoots, guava flowers.
        The child is eating the earth, learning
        the first lessons again, tasting where we're from.

Young Farmer at a Roadside Stand

In the heartland, the dust hasn't settled,
the history of place continually reshapes itself—
    a windblown spirit inhabits the plains and valleys
    mingled with generations of farmers who,
    on the same acreage, send their ancestral taproots
        deep into the soil.

On a gentle rise at the south end of the farm
stone markers of a family cemetery jut like faces
    in the distance,
jagged letters carved deep in stone;
polished and weathered names like Jedediah and Mary,
Ezra and Rebecca, who tended this same earth,
gathered wood from trees along the same river that flows
beside the farm today. The bones and spirit of family rest here
    in the gentle rolling countryside.

From the electrified barn in this rural Ohio swath of green,
the saxophone jazz from a radio floats out over the quiet landscape,
a young husky man carries a pail to an adjacent shed.
    He has a pierced ear
    and his girlfriend has a rose tattoo on her ankle
    and another leafy green and red swirl on her shoulderblade.

White boxed beehives stacked at the edge of the clover field,
honey for sale at the road side.

    The young man, reaching for change,
    says he is as comfortable sitting at the computer
    as he is driving the combine
    over a hundred acres in the summer heat.
    He could leave it all behind.

He's not impressed in knowing more about bees and honey
than most of his contemporaries. There is another kind of lure

out beyond the willow wind break
that his great grandfather planted along the river.
He says he would always come back and visit,
                not go too far away,
          but he could leave it all behind.
          Something in the air pulls him, tests his attachment
          to this place where he has been since birth—
          all his world is not here, as it was for his grandparents.

Still, the blade of grass he has in his mouth tastes sweeter
than any comfort that he might find in town.
His world, much wider than the world inhabited
by those ancestors buried on the hill,
is shaped and reshaped by their having been here, and he knows
as deeply as they did, that he can never really leave this place.

Visual Healing

In his twelve years the young boy knew his own suffering,
learned that while his friends played and shouted outdoors
he was being educated on the growth of tumors,
learned how painful and sick he was losing clumps of hair
spending days in bed as the seasons changed
outside the window.

For him it was the cowboys and Indians in battle,
for others it was a less distinct cool blue glow
surrounding and absorbing the hot points, and for others still
it was the image of hands carrying away the unneeded toxins
in the body. They all had their visual model of healing—
lifting, absorbing, surrounding, and subduing the runaway guests,
the invaders, the fast-growing balls of heat.

The young boy and his new friends at the cancer clinic
learned that the invaders were inseparable from themselves,
even if it seemed like warfare in the territory
of their bodies by something apart from it.
The colors and hot and cool points swirled within the galaxy
of one's own body, not invaders from space.
Some of the drama could be re-scripted, they learned.

The young boy learned that his visual healing gave him strength
far beyond that needed to kick a ball or swing a bat,
which he would learn to do later if he liked.
He learned that tumors shrink and recede, become dormant,
and conceal themselves in hidden caves.
At twelve he learned that the pictures in his head
changed the body, changed the world,
and he could choose to participate and guide his pictures
for his own healing.

It was, for him, like changing the seasons
from winter to spring.

Blue Venezuelan Sky

In our haste to get away, we had no time
   to make a home—

we contented ourselves, instead,
   with a quickly thatched nest
constructed
among the dry thorns
     of the Ocotillo

this would be
our desert retreat

while racing in the sun
     toward some reward
     awaiting us, impatient,

not resting long enough
     for the tears
     to dry beneath our feet

when explosions
     pounded in our ears
and the memories of peeling paint
from all the familiar buildings
     of our restless childhood
     crumbled again

brick dust angels
     glistening in the sun
     telling us to believe
     that this time would be different
and these wicked dreams would end

at dawn's first light.

Life in Slab City

In the wake of decommissioning,
the U.S. military base
became unrecognizable—
where once the discipline of schedules
and regulations guided the day,
now hundreds of ghostly slabs of concrete
baked in the desert sun
until the arrival of the first vagabonds
seeking a free space
and a new way of living.

A small flat slab,
        not a section
        or an acre,
but a little square space on which
        to pile one's meager possessions

not a Brook Farm or a communal experiment,
but one family or one individual at a time,
setting up a truck, a bus,
a recreational vehicle on its last legs
confined to a space, a kind of new home.

Individualism became a social mix
of dreamers, artists, tired dropouts,
and young and old outcasts from
the dominant society that could no longer
impose its constraints on daily life
among the slab dwellers.

If anarchism is self-governance,
what was this social organism
in Slab City?

Now, 50 years into life
in Slab City,
Amazon Prime delivery trucks
bring the cardboard kindling
for the trash-burning fires
and the plastic wrapping
that drapes the dried desert plants
like colored banners glinting in the breeze.

Mountain Lion

One time they netted the wild cat,
another time it was the tranquilizer gun

For a long time the mountain lion wore a collar
        or a narrow metal tag
                piercing the soft ear.

It had been a mistake to leave the cover
        of the forest and take the easy trail
                through open country

where first they spotted it
        in their binoculars.

When the collar batteries failed
        after several months,
                the tracking collar fell off.

By then they knew its 500-mile route
        from central California to Mexico
                over mountain ridges

seeking deer for meals
        avoiding the fences and walls
                and the long unbroken lanes
                of freeways, aqueducts, and roadways.

Then the dart
        and dizziness

and while it lay in a drowsy state
        the trackers inspected teeth with calipers,
                weighed the limp body on their scales,

and set the once-wild animal in the shade
        until it stumbled away
                out of its slumber.

Once the lions roamed the continent,
        food supply and water source plentiful,
        then the poachers hunted them down
                for sport, for bounty,
                        a pelt for display.

Now the world is closing in,
        more days without food,
                more difficulty finding a mate
                in the long journey
        searching for hidden springs or a quiet place to rest.

Peripatetic, transient, never far from the maw
        of urban traps,

they try to avoid the modern sights and sounds
        and stay far away from
                the slow tightening
                of the choke collar.

Whispering Cottonwoods
(In memory of my sister)

If I said the bare cottonwoods in the moonlit winter night
looked like long fingers pointing upward, seeking something,
would you follow my thought in silence
to her hospital bed two months ago
when her warm bony fingers rested weightless in my hand?

How could you know I'm not thinking of the cottonwoods,
or the glazed snow under moonlight,
but instead absorbing myself in those last hours with her?

We conceal worlds within our silences,
or behind the brief whispered utterances.

When she became too tired to speak, I washed her hands
with a warm wash cloth, hands that I then knew
would never grow wrinkled with old age.

We did not discuss death, hope, or regret
during those precious days
of lingering lucidity.
We let those hours slip by.

So much of what's real remains silent
so much of what could have been said
will remain forever unspoken.

Continents of meaning never to be uncovered.
We talked, instead, of the commonplace
and forgettable details of the moment.

There were opportunities to try to unravel how it came
to this, the slipping away of it all.
We said "I love you" to each other,
and maybe that is enough.

The nurses came for blood, for pulse, for a distraction.

A week after I returned home across the country
   she sighed her last breath alone,
   leaving a half smile for her mother and father.

I will sit beneath the cottonwoods in the coming summer,
   hear her fading laughter, and count her first birthday missed,
   without a word to anyone.

The Last Visit

You will know the preciousness
        of the moment

        when it has passed.

That is the way it works—
        protecting and shielding you
                from the unbearable pain
                        of knowing
                that each moment
                is unrepeatable and unique.

The lace window curtains
        gently swaying or resting still against the painted sill
        the smell of the pillow case
                oiled by a once-warm head

                or the shaft of afternoon sunlight
                streaming golden through the dust motes
                of a vacated room.

For months and years after the events have passed
        the images will visit you, unbeckoned in the night,
        and remind you that none of what you have witnessed
        in this life of gains and losses, births and deaths,
                will ever again be repeated.

One time is all you get.
        One instant.
                One smile across the room,
                        one embrace at the closing door,

        and it's gone . . .
                as you walk down the hall alone.

You will want to have another chance
            to do it over . . . differently.

You would do anything
        to be again
            in the presence of love.

A New Poetry of Wonder

Today a tearful Wordsworth
paid a visit and spoke to me
of a new poetry of the stars

his overflowing emotion
recollected not in tranquility
but from a bewildering turbulence
of seeing distant galaxies and nebulae
that he was not prepared to see.

Returning earlier in the day to the cottage
from his resting place among the swaying daffodils
he had gazed upon images
recently transmitted from
the James Webb Space Telescope
and he asked,
"How far is a billion light years?"

When his pleurisy recently became disabling
the fMRI peered deep within
the branching bronchioles of his lungs, displaying
to his disbelieving mind
microtubules that were not observable two centuries ago
when he asked his personal physician
         to make a house call.

In today's science of wonder
he sees new sources of art,
vast regions and opportunities for the poet's sensitive eye,

"But human footprints on the moon?" he asked,
shaking his downcast head,
and one could almost see the romance
         slowly leaking from his heart.

Vivid Dreams, Antarctica

I.
Dearest love,

Here Man Ray photographs Matisse
        for an audience—
and Brassai, the "eye of Paris,"
sets up his camera
for a nightlife scene at the base of Mt. Erebus—
misty clouds swirling
        around bowler hats
                suspended in space

        hovering above base camp
invitations posted: The Surrealist Ball
                         This Saturday Night
                         on the Ross Sea ice shelf . . .

White rabbits the size of caribou
turn to confetti,
all photographs are impounded,
marked NOT FOR EXPORT

"No one will believe the vivid dreams
        these folks are having down here"
—the only radio message sneaked out—

Emanations from the polar caps
planetary forces—we must be all right, my love.
This is what we must believe.

II.
Dearest Love—

Great Paleolithic band of wanderers here
                            this week
just passing through, like us,
visiting and talking around the fire—
rumors of warm underground lakes further on
                    forests and brown bears
                    beyond the distant ridge

This is no experiment, I heard someone say,
frozen beard breaking in his lap.
Another, wrapped in blue gortex
cried salty tears, fogging up his helmet.
What tribe is this?
Where is home? Wilderness?
There must be a return,
        we all sobbed—
        a ceremony of weeping,
                cleansing and purifying us
                for the real trial.

We'll be all right, said our letter carrier,
returning, again, my latest letter to you.

III.
Dearest love,

        Spectral hieroglyphics—
                positively dazzling . . .

The sea of love
        is frozen again today;
There will NO BATHING signs posted
                at the top of ice sheets
                1500 feet high,

roads dynamited up to the heights
        where we perch like space-age penguins
facing the sun
sitting like Buddhas
in a row
at peace for this eternal moment.
One of the penguins turned to me and said,
"This is the real world."
We all hallucinate together here.
        Good band of friends.
        This, they say, is how cultures start.

IV.
Leariest Dove,

A reindeer leapt,
        and took a bite out of the moon

Mad for love, leaving the world out of joint
                        —off kilter—
There are scouts
in geosynchronous orbit
        watching our every move from above
                —a celestial panoptic eye
        scoping us out, checking us twice
        something something something
        whether we're naughty or nice . . .

There'll be no Santa in this winter dreamscape
        Kurtz he dead
        Curtsie and goo-night, Bill
        Goo-night Loo
        Goo-night   Goo-night.

The Oldest Irishman

The oldest Irishman in the village
      lay deathly ill—
      his three surviving sons,
            now all old themselves,
      were gathered round
            the oldest Irishman's bedside
                  when they weren't playing cards at the table
                  and sipping a pint "to keep up the spirits."
                  There was money, too, on the table.

The oldest Irishman in the village,
      scion of a long family branch
            known for gambling
            and a joyful knack for supporting the local economy
                at Malloy's hotel bar,
                insisted that he was not as deathly ill
                as the villagers claimed.
                He even winked when he said,
                "Make you a wager."

The oldest son heard his father rightly,
      and no sooner had the idea planted itself,
      the oldest son was talking to his brothers
            at the card table
            over a cool tonic.
      "The old man wants to place a bet that he
      will outlive the scoundrels in town.
      But more to our purpose, what do you say
      we see which of us is the most clairvoyant
      in determining the date of decease for the old man?"

Preparations were made for the "Tourney" as the brothers called it.
            Ground rules were established (and written down)
            The selected dates were written on paper and placed
            in the urn that lay on the old mahogany mantelpiece.

The first and most important ground rule they agreed on:
they could offer assistance to the old man,
as they might in curling,
to bring about a favorable result
and a chance to win.

When the sons told the old man about the wager
and the high stakes,
he winked and said he wanted in,
and they all laughed.

Part II: Glimpses

Perseverance Furthers

Drop by drop,
from the leaky faucet in the kitchen, tiny echoes
      fill the night.

By morning,
cool clear water
      brims the pot
           in overflowing abundance.

In the rocky Himalayan highlands,
barefoot monks step lightly
during their daily walking meditation.
After weeks and months and years
their soft silent stepping
has turned the stones beneath their feet
      to powder—
      a straight line of white chalk dust
      fine enough to drift in air currents
           across oceans and continents.

Weave together the glimpses of dreams,
      and the remembered snatches of conversation;
Work the thoughts like tumbled stones,
      smoothing the once rough edges.
Time will bring life into your words.

Triptych

1. Preparing for a Public Talk

Here it goes again.
I can see one of the judges on the panel
asking me after my talk
on Ecology, Zen, and Responsibility,
"What is Zen?"
and me with a stupid grin
breaking a pencil and tossing the
pieces into the air over my shoulder,
the way I did in English class in '67
when Mr. Youngerman asked the same question
after my report on Suzuki and Watts—
and Allan Graubard clapped his hands and laughed aloud.

2. Smart Bugs

The tiny spittle-bug
is an intelligent creature
housing itself in a gob of spit.
Who would think of looking there
for trouble, or for a meal?

When I entered
Colorado Springs at the end
of a long day
driving in hot summer
about '69
I parked the little VW bug
late at night between two other cars
in a used car lot—
well-lighted and safe.
In the morning, well rested,
I drove away before business opened.

3. Impermanences

Getting older now,
forgetting what it was
that troubled me in youth

Cold point of snow flake
melting on cheek

Fading light at nightfall

In Amber

Sealed in amber, fellow traveler, you
will outlast my dust when it is all said
                    and done;

Your curved spine, still pliant
one would guess, after a hundred million years,
resting inside a golden chamber
that will preserve you
until insects again reign on this worn earth.

The fossilized remnants of my species
will contain the heaviest metals we could mine
and synthesize, outlasting our strongest bones,
buried deep in canisters so no eye would look upon
their painful promise that change
and rapid mutation
are encapsulated inside
our death chambers.

The seed that flies over the seas, resting
its paper wings on the waves
before flying away again
on the warm currents of air,
contains in it all that is needed for earth and water
to transform it into full-grown tree or vine
or vibrant flower clinging to a rocky windswept crag.

Contained in the cocoon, the interim
of life that passes from land to air.
Pods of life, carrying all the travelers to other places,
journeys without destination, unfolding change,
grabbing hold of life in a new home of sun and wind.

There will be remote galaxies
visited by my species in the years to come,
but could those travelers ever return with anything as beautiful
as your webbed wing magnified in amber, a reminder
of what exists no more,
the wisp of life's golden glow on this earth.

No Beginning

Here
at the conjunction of this in-breath
and the constellation of galaxies
swirling in their ever-widening expanse,

the universe breathes
                me.

Every arising moment
emerging from its own precondition.

No beginnings.

. . . the originating breath
        the seed of consciousness
        out of the silence and nothingness
                    grows.

The mad monk of the village
patiently tells me not to search for origins;
tracks in the snow will not lead me
to the clouds that brought the snowfall.
He tells me that all the world is in this moment.

No beginnings.

Touch this solid clod of earth, smell
the oily rich resin in the pine needles
at your feet, some voice tells me.
The mad monk of the village
taps his walking stick on a rock.
Listen, he says.

This imaginative place within the solid flux
that conjures up a distant village and

its attendant monk . . . the intersection
of mind and the hard ground I walk on.

Here in this valley carved by glaciers
where dampness rolls off the grass
on these warm summer mornings—how could this place
give rise to the mad monk of the village in my head?
There are no beginnings.

Recognitions and awakenings, imagining a beginning in a universe
becoming conscious of itself.
Stepping forward now
unraveling patience
tapping a few stones along the way
in the bright warm sun . . .
the smell of leaves on the wind.

Autumn

The earth is turning its sunburnt cheek
toward our eyes, showing its deepest red foliage
at the tops of maples, the wide-awake yellows
filling our field of vision in the birch groves,
pulling the sap inward for another season.

Has it been a year already, we ask each other
on our ride through the mountains
to catch the fading sun on these shortened days.
When we were young we lay for hours in the dry
mouldering piles of crackling leaves, our rakes
leaned against the trunks of trees, we laughing and
telling stories that we would never again remember
or tell. What we remember is the smell of earth
in those leaves and how we felt so much alive
in those bright piles of season's end.

And today, too, we stop and wade ankle-deep
in the still-bright leaves gathered on the forest floor,
seeing our breath in the morning sunlight air,
removing a leafy fragment from our hair, brushing off
twigs that hold to us, and we talk again about things of
little consequence in the presence of a world too big
for us to understand, cradled in its last warm leaves of the season.

Beneath It All

Let us say that
beneath the surface of our gregarious lives
there are numerous haunting voices and straining faces awaiting us.
The sights and sounds of the nightmare of loneliness
patiently gathering
within the culmination of our loves—
> and at the end of the long road of learning and living,
> behind all the tastes of love along the way,
> the world of pain awaits us.

All the accumulations and cultivations, the nurturings
of friendships and relations, the loves and sorrows;
the acquisitions of patience, the losses of memory
and strivings, and all the attachments to wanting and being
wanted . . .

> All the building up
> wears down.

Let us suppose that we are willing to let all that go
by the time we see the final light narrowing
into a spindle of faint unfocused light,
and feel the last heat running out of our bones.

Is that eternal silence that spreads its wings from both sides
of our lives—before and after—
> —that silence that calls us back—
> is that all there is . . .
> punctuated only by these brief decades
> that slip by?

I'd like to think not—
to say instead that these are some of the lessons learned,
> some of the preliminary notes taken
> for what will follow.

But then again . . .
perhaps this moment now is all there is, and
that the curse for being born into a world of time
is that we are continually tempted to forget the present.

But this all seems too much the real thing;
that there's no show after this brief dress rehearsal.
When the lights go dim,
and all the sounds end at the final fade-out,
      other actors continue to enter the crowded stage
      and the play goes on . . .
                      for them.

How much more to learn in this flicker of light
between two eternal darknesses.

Chuang Tzu and the Culture of Appropriate Suffering

Chuang Tzu cried and sobbed alone when his wife died;
he did not display his mourning in public,
and when he had paid his respects to his wife
and the life they had shared for many years,
he beat on his pots and pans,
drumming through the night,
carrying on loudly, annoying the neighbors
who thought how disrespectful of a man whose wife had just died.

He should go into silent retreat, they thought;
he should remain downcast and solemn for some time
to display the proper degree of suffering.

When asked how he could be so disrespectful and playful
with death still in the air, Chuang Tzu said that he had mourned
naturally at his wife's death, and for a time he was saddened,
but how much more disrespectful it would have been to her
for him to carry on selfishly in his own grief, he said.
For her, too, he would get on with his life,
for he would not be mourning if she was with him;
why should he mourn for his own loneliness
when they had so many pleasant years together.
What was to be gained from prolonging the sorrow and self pity?

How disrespectful it would have been
to do anything other than experience joy in this life
and show it by beating on his pots and pans,
drumming through the night.

Sand Painting

Gather a handful of ochre stone
    from the vein on the mountain
    across the valley,
grind it with mortar and pestle
to smooth chalk the color of the back of your hand
    in fading sunlight,
and place the powder in a jar until all the colors
    for the sand painting are thus gathered.

Find the white of rib-bone in the desert mesa
where thousands of years have been pressed into
    a sliver that runs like the path of meteorites
    angled down into the earth
        from the wedge of mountain;
    scrape the hard whiteness with your fingernails
    rubbing it into the thimbleful of white that will
        be in the northern skull.

All day for seven days
gather and grind the deposits of rock
from this desert valley and mountain home,
assembling them for the mandala
where heart and mind join in vision—
symbols of the ancestors,
colors and signs,
a cosmology of meaning manifested in dust.

Impermanence and tradition
shared in the sand painting, days of quiet attention,
each movement and gesture ceremonial,
rooted in wisdom of the past
like the grain of mineral blue
flecked in the mountainside, hidden beneath the overhang
    of ledges;

At the end of days, the work is done, the connection between
the earth's colors and the passing moment linked;

wipe the sand painting from its recognized patterns
       and symbols
       into undifferentiated unity again, gather the sand
in a cloth satchel, carry it back to the overhang,
and release it into the wind, or into the river, returning it
to mingle again with the elements.

The Mad Monk of the Mountain

Give him a name, because he will not
come down to tell us.
He has no need of us, it appears.
Can you imagine! Solitary fool, living apart
from community, from all that we know
today about our world.

I see him walking the hillsides, the meadows,
fishing and collecting berries in summer,
gathering wood in fall,
walking, bundled in rags, in winter.

What goes through a madman's mind
so far from the movement of our village
and commerce of human life?
The villagers say he sometimes laughs when he is alone,
a dangerous thing for the mind.
He talks to trees and flowers.
He bathes in water too cold for his own good.

He sits long wasteful hours, doing nothing, the useless creature,
wasting away with his eyes closed, tattered robe blowing
         in the wind.
He has no family, the poor fool, tapping on rocks
with his walking stick, reciting poems on the windy mountaintops,
like some kind of carefree mountain goat.

Yellow Potted Flower

Do not offer consolation
>   to the flower
>   that opens only in the morning
>   and closes its petals through the day.

Do not remind the flower
>   what it is missing
>   at the sun's zenith
>   or what the long summer day displays
>   to those who witness it.

Marvel instead at the mystery
>   of its modest display
>   and be present
>   when it welcomes you at dawn.

Its grass-like leaves and narrow stem
>   emerge from bulb
>   growing skyward
>   following the course
>   of its own adaptations.

It has restrained its urges
>   to grow like the others
>   and makes no demands
>   for special soils or light.

Setting Out

"I have forgotten why I came here," she said.
"It has been so long since I set out with a few provisions
        and good intentions,
then losing direction, stumbling off the path."

So many detours along the way,
        obstructions, obstacles
        plans deferred, lives put on hold.

This is what people do;
        this is what we tell ourselves.

Then we meet people in new places
        who point to guideposts in all directions;
        they say:
        we go on
        we stumble
        we pass through it

There is no straight line
        from where we are
        to where we will be

We must go on;
this too is what people have always done

you may be pulled by the outgoing tide
or by some ancestral migrational impulse,
        or by desires for a new beginning.

But once you step into the stream, they say,
there is no choice but to flow with it
        or be swept away.

Listening to the Wind

A friend of mine once said all experience
       can teach us,
and asked me to imagine what the world was like
before I was born—
           not the world of history
      and all the incarnations of life from
           swirling organic matter, or
           the world of family ancestors
      and generations upon generations of evolving
           humans—

but, instead, to imagine a complete and total lack
of my own consciousness,
and to project that infinitely before my birth
and infinitely after my death.

      What does that do, she asked,
           to your sense of the time you
               have in this life.

This life, from innocence to pain, with joy and enough sorrow
      to make it seem interminable at times,
      and eternally precious at others,
      . . . this life, seen as the fantastic set of circumstances that
      conspired to bring consciousness from nothingness . . . and
           return it again some day
           to the same unchanging nothingness,
      is only occasionally appreciated as the chance occasion
           that it is.

My friend said,
      Think of never having been . . .

      No thought at all . . .

No presence . . . not even the thought of galaxies
                    without you.

            Not even the thought of emptiness itself.
                    Try to imagine such a void.

Those words of hers
        come back to me
                when I am not trying to bring them back—

        as if to coax me toward some understanding
                before it all vanishes again;
                to soothe me into accepting the inevitable
                        that we all come to know,
                        for having entered into the world of time.

Looking Seaward

In the bright light
slight right of where we stand
looking to sea
over scalloped waves,
we see islands of dolphins
bobbing in curves of shiny gray,
arcing beyond our reach.

We marvel at their seaward gestures
from our sandy cove,
feet planted firmly.

Once that was our home, too,
aqueous, evanescent—

there was coral for our backbones
in the food-rich sea . . .

What sea monsters
drove us from sea to tree tops?

Legless sea elephants, manatees
sprouted legs in the estuaries

sea lettuce growing
          on trees

sirens calling the sea-dwellers landward

until their feet
were firmly planted,
          yearning for seaward buoyancy.

What the Dolphins Taught Me

Remember to breathe.

The Great Detachment

When language brought us closer
        and fire pulled us in
        we removed ourselves further
        from the old familiar contacts

Our elders tell us
        we became estranged from the plants and animals
        that accompanied us
        in our early learning.

The tree, the antelope, the sun
        were transformed into words,
        substitutions for what they had been before words,
        and this kept them at a distance.

The image, the memory, the pictographs we drew
        on the shale cliffsides
        became the new markers
        of our separateness,
        the growing distance
        from what had once been part of us.

We did not know then that such advances
        as language and fire
        would someday
        detach generations
        from who they once were;

That words and what they pointed to
        would be misunderstood
        and the little linguistic fissures and cracks
        that emerged among us
        would become vast chasms
        that no language could repair.

And only when we trampled our fellow travelers underfoot
and buried them with words of indifference
did we glimpse how far we had wandered
into the wilderness of our undoing.

Language Arising from the Sea

As we lost our language
      we began to lose the feelings
      associated with words
            until we let go of the thoughts
            and the string of memories
                        and then the wispy pictures
                        no longer moored
                        to the habits of the mind.

For a long time we hung on to phrases
      as though they kept their meaning
      when they were strung out like drying laundry
            blowing around the wooden clothespins
            keeping them from snapping
                        in our heads
                        as the connections
                        drifted into thin air.

With the dropping away of meaning
      we stared for a long while
      to the sea where a single repeating tonal chant
            reminded us of the living breath
            that pulsed around the planet
                        where the oceans
                        shouldered the constant
                        nudging of the current

            as we listened to the source
                  of our language and strivings.

We Hear You Now, Victor Jara

You gave the people your voice
      and today they carry the words
          inside of them
          singing quietly
      in groups of two and three and four

You can see in their untrusting eyes
      the source of their muted song

the barely audible hum in one
      becomes anthemic in the many
          who sing today with Victor Jara

they may take away the hands
      or smash the instruments of music
      but the voices rise up
      from deep inside
      first faint, then like distant thunder
      until the words themselves become recognizable
      and their meaning painfully burned
          into the hearts of people

and passed on to another generation
      able to raise their fists high into the air

accompaniment to their loud and everlasting voices

Riding the Fiction

When we lived in the fiction, we heard voices say,
"We knew then that we were in for
      one of Marlow's interminable tales,"
and sure enough Marlow's voice rises out of the misty fog
saying that these lands were once primitive, and he unmasks
      the big lie of the civilizing influence
      of occupation and colonization.

The fictive influence on living
      leads one to believe so entirely
      in the story that has been building
      for decades and reinforced by habit
            that it appears almost incomprehensible that
            there could have been any other way for events
            (and influences) to go

and now the story has a forward momentum of its own
      and we are guided through days
            that didn't seem to be of our own choosing,
            but instead were planned and scripted elsewhere,
                  and rolled out for us to ride . . . effortlessly.

In the time required for the tide to turn,
      Marlow spins his tale
      of civilization's thin veneer, a light carapace
      that cracks when social support dissolves
      and the potential for self-governing
      collapses into self indulgence, the will to power,
      and a worship of the self.

We live in the fiction, including those we fashion for ourselves,
      and now and then another fictive voice
      will step on our welcome mat and present a tale
      that illuminates for us a glimpse of the way
            we are living our lives.

The fictive is real—as real as any influence—
    and we tune our receivers
    for signals that will bring us comfort . . .
        . . . and keep the veneer pliable, mirror-like
        for at least another day.

Graffiti Art

On freeway overpasses, sides of boxcar trains,
abandoned stores, and the backs of old markets,
the swirling colors of night-time art,
rapid and secret fast-drying paint

messages from a moving generation
a flight of passing moments transient, in flight

a street-long mural, almost iridescent,
a people's history, hardship and heartache,
and pride of staking a claim on the run,
accumulating and gathering status
finding ways to decorate all the surfaces,
          voices invisible
gaining legitimacy and a public following

photo albums filling with the record of images
before the walls are white-washed
to conceal the colorful challenges
          by voices that speak with pride
          in the neighborhood.

Palimpsests of paint, layers of Monet and Picasso
covered by the new signatures
of local artists with no museum
but the streets, the bare walls
where no streetlights illuminate the message.

City-scape canvases of concrete
in the outdoor studio

where tomorrow another work is on display
sometimes just a hurried scrawl
and at other times a temporary masterpiece
      for only a few eyes to see
      before the exhibit moves on to other places.

Modern pictographs depicting with haiku speed
all that can be contained in an instant.

In the Light of the Full Moon

In the light of the full moon
        some flecks of mica on the road glint and sparkle;
        some jagged stones reach deeper into a wounded earth;
           all the stones illuminate our way
           along the moonlit roadway.

In the light of the full moon
        the poetry of wonder and awe
        pulls the tides of curiosity,
           unveiling mysteries, insights—
        looks to the stars beyond the bright-lit moon,
        bends the arc of thought and contemplation
           to rest on the impossible,
           pondering some unanswerable question.

In the light of the full moon
        the glimpse is what we get;
        the curtain of night highlights the incompleteness
           of our vision.

In the light of the full moon
        we look upward to the orb
        reflecting our own inner light
           from the sun source
           whose presence remains hidden
           from the moon-struck looker.

At daybreak, the light of the full moon
        is too faint to be seen,
        evaporated in the sun's glow,
           gone again from source of awe
           to non-presence,
           being swept back into the cycle
               of appearance and non-appearance.

And creative forces swirl
    into existence
    new patterns, waves, vibrations

    and under an illuminated moon
    someone conjures into existence
    a reflection, a glimpse, a glimmer.

Pattern Seekers

For a time we contemplated the patterns
        of our ancestral migration
        before the continents divided;

from early stick markings in sand
        to elaborate paintings in caves
        we discovered in time that we are pattern seekers

animal footprints, serrated leaves, and night-time stars
        captivated us; we stared at the ocean waves,
        sunsets, and wood fires.

Eventually, we came to learn about
        the interrelatedness of things:

In the cross-section cut of burl wood
        we saw the unmistakable pattern
        of swirling stellar nebulae
        fanning outward like growth rings of the universe

chlorophyll and blood share metallic elements
        as hemoglobin crosses the barrier
        of plant and animal,
        concealing their intermingling
        long ago

the alluvial fan pattern of river delta
        appears again in the palm leaf
        and in wind-blown sand dunes

and with enough time the rocks do become trees
        life emerges from decay
        and we sit again in wonder that we are here at all,
        privileged observers of this unfolding moment.

Finding a Way

We practiced first in our dreams
        so we wouldn't fall to the ground
        or be seen floundering in public

levitation exercises
        night after night
        in the privacy of our darkness

perfecting the style
        becoming weightless
        learning to soar someday
        like The Flying Wallendas

without net or supporting wires

we tried to live in a world
        without gravity

        without being pulled down
        by the everydayness

for a time we tried to become invisible,
        venture out without notice

and in this way we learned
        the lessons from our dreams

Woodmaker's Bowl

The sound of mallet and chisel
wood on wood
against wood

> The craftsman seated outside the shed
> speaking intermittently with his wife
> standing nearby

flecks and shavings
falling to the ground in a pile
of soft papery curls.

> A few unrushed words exchanged, occasional smiles
> man and wife knowing
> each other's comfort with silence

The original wood block
reshapen by subtraction—
revealing a bowl

its most useful part—the space
scooped out, hollowed
where the displaced shavings
were extracted
from the fine-grained, tight-fibered
block of wood

> The silences chiseled from years of words
> conveying meaning
> the eyes picking up where the words left off
> in the craft and art of communicating

the bowl rests silently on the table

> clasped hands on the walk back to the house.

A New Season of Love

In the season of love
      there were flowers
      and we remember tall grasses too

      clouds like wispy cotton
           against a deepest blue sky
           from horizon to wooded horizon

      a blanket and basket
           food to nourish the love
           that comes when we're present

      appreciative of the dissolving cloud
           knowing that what has passed
           has beauty too

We do not think so much
           of such
           matters now,
as the season of love matures
           into a rich contentment

           that the most beautiful sky
                arrives at sunset.

What Is Poetry?

Some will want to hear political astuteness
  or a cry for freedom
  when it seems the least possible.

Some will applaud the loud and flashy
  in-your-face stun-gun kind of feel.

Some will pine for the triumph
  of love over darkness and decline;
  they may croon for a love lyric
  that will soothe the pain for a moment;
    maybe even give a smile.

There may be those who demand a rhyme
  they can dance to
  and if you don't deliver
  you can dance by yourself for awhile
    and see how that goes.

And there may be some among us who see the sparkle
  that glows from self-expression
  in all its faces of human
    —and inhuman—interaction.

And at some point, perhaps one person, and then another,
  allows an inner insight to come out
  to share a deep human impulse
  to burrow deep into the unknown
  and return with the story of a quest, maybe even
  an invitation to a way of being
    that connects us with deeper
    archetypes that bind us together.

  Or, the insight may be about enjoying some plums
    from the refrigerator.

On the Way to Somewhere

alien outside
always the visitor
since leaving the first home
and learning later
that home is different than place of origin

Just a transient passing through
        for a lifetime.

A brief stop can become decades
of living with the illusion that a long stop is a home;
in the end the long stopover, too, is transitory.

And what then when you live without
        the homeward return?

What do you do with nationalism
that keeps the world's refugees out;
like trying to stop a tidal wave
        that returns again with greater force?

With the outsider view,
the alien sees the way indoctrination works,
the way any Winston Smith would know.
Its signs are ubiquitous, in the open
        for everyone to see but no longer notice.

The population displays appearances
        of confidence and comfort
        while masking a fragility, a vulnerability—
        a fear that the thin veneer of civility
                will crack under the strain
        if their present way of life doesn't continue
                or improve
        requiring acquisition of products

depletion of global resources . . .
and finding that there are limits to growth after all.

And the alien sees that there is no safe place to go
where it doesn't feel like another temporary stop
on the way to somewhere.

Intelligence in This Unfurling Moment

Aspen grove, a single organism,
       a community appearing as separate trees,
       leaves quaking in the well-watered hillside
       growing where the valley's nutrients
       will last hundreds of years.

Underground mycelium communities
       spreading nodes of communication
       in mats of subterranean fungal forest
       adapted to the mild earthy conditions.

Tropical cutter ants following the scent
       for the task they perform;
       no one in charge as the work gets done—
       chopping, transporting, building their city of tunnels,
       working for the benefit of the community
       that they cannot see from their own local vantage point.

A global network of human brains
       advancing without conscious direction;
       a complex organization of connections
       working out what it is going to be in its corner of the galaxy.

Cells awaiting differentiation
       awaiting the code assignments for specialization
       of what they will become.

We glimpse with awe the self-organizing intelligence
       all around and within us; observing for a moment
       our illusory separateness—

       being pulled by self-governing momentum
       toward some understanding that awaits us,
       awareness already contained in this unfurling moment.

Bountiful Wisdom

In the illusion of awakening
        we called our confusions
        Wisdom Stories

growing confident
        with each retelling
        we began to believe
        we were getting closer
        to an understanding

confirmed by our instruments
        everything pointing in the right direction
        selecting the details
        that confirmed what we sought to see

we developed techniques
        that suited our times

we peeled away misunderstandings
        of the past

we gathered in ever larger groups
        to convince ourselves
        that we could uncover
        universal truths

and while we lived in apparent relative comfort
        we concealed our private unspoken doubts

and when each of us grew old,
        bodies breaking down,
        minds growing frail,
        we forgot all that we had written
        in books that withered with us
        into obscurity

not even knowing by then
      that this decay is the truth
      we needed to know
      but kept forgetting

Part III: Reflections

Where Are the Crows?

Today, waiting for the morning bus, I saw crows fly overhead;
some were reflected in the second-floor windows
of the building across the street from the bus stop.

The windows reflected birds and morning clouds,
the cool glass muted by a thin dusty film.

I saw black crows reflected against a dark November sky.

In the same window later that morning
someone may have looked through at the rain glistening in the street
or saw from that other side of the glass the candlelight reflected
against the warm interior walls of the room.

The same window, resting there, reflecting
different changing worlds for those who look into it.

With a small adjustment of the eye
one sees not the reflection,
        maybe not the film on the glass
                maybe not the window at all,

maybe the viewer looks through it.

At times reflective, at others transparent,
the window depends on the focus of the observing eye.

The window was not troubled by the darkening sky,
nor observant of the passing crows, not dreamy about the
flickering warm candlelight, not speculative about the levels of mind
or the relations of sight and insight.

The window is just the window
and it will be there tomorrow, reflecting the sky
as I wait for the bus.

Cultivating the Art of Wonder

Wonder at any age
will sustain us
when we are overcome by the mystery of what is outside of ourselves
waiting and watching in awe, enthralled
      as a child
      by the blade of grass or an anthill,
or in old age
by the warmth of sun on cheek and browning arm.

From wonder and curiosity
comes the inflow of knowledge
and the unspooling of understanding,
an effortless and all-consuming art
in pursuit of disciplined devotion.

Some will make music for the heart,
others will transform paint and clay
      into pleasures for the eyes,
and others, still, will take their lifetime of wonder
and fashion it, in time, into a thing of beauty,

      making it possible for others
      to be awe-struck, inspired for a moment
      through the artist's eye.

Rock Art Impermanence

I sent a text message to Marlene with a photo of "rock art" on Ventura Beach. It was an image of two artfully constructed cairns about two feet high consisting of delicately stacked stones of different sizes balanced carefully. A passing woman commented that she enjoyed seeing the new groups of balanced stones each time she came to the beach but that she had never observed anyone constructing them. I said, that's what makes them mysterious. A community of people who never meet each other, contributing to a shared project.

For a time I stood nearby and watched the ocean and the sea birds in the late afternoon sun. Then, I heard the sound of stick against stone and turned to see a young boy about 10 years of age knocking down one of the carefully balanced stacks of rounded stones. He continued swinging and striking the stones, knocking them to the sand as his father and little brother looked on.

The ocean, too, is a powerful entropic force, tumbling large boulders into smoothly rounded rocks, stones, pebbles, and fine grains of sand. I stared for some time at the father, then turned back to the sea and the incessant pounding of the waves on the rocky shoreline. I thought about there being people, some of whom are builders and some who break things down. A little while later a group of more than a dozen young boys and girls and adults arrived and sat nearby after observing the one remaining stack of stones, not knowing that moments earlier there had been two—and the one that had been knocked over was the more impressive and intricately arranged of the two. The children and adults sat in a semi-circle and it appeared that they were on a kind of field trip, learning about the beach and coming to appreciate what the beach had to offer.

I walked on, having taken my photo, and remembered the moment in J. D. Salinger's short story "Teddy" where young Teddy observes through the porthole of the cruise ship he is on with his family that someone above has thrown orange peels overboard and for that brief moment while they floated on the surface and then disappeared, he realized that the only place they now existed was in his mind—in his memory. That woman on the beach, and I, appreciated what many people had constructed, and for the young boy it was a kind of sport to swing his stick at the stones and knock them down. Perhaps a Tibetan Taoist would see impermanence in this scene, much like the colorful sand mandalas that they take days to patiently construct, only to sweep the sand into a bag and pour the contents into the sea or a river.

In the evening, while renaming the digital image of the photo I had taken of the balanced stones, I did something that inadvertently deleted the image. Meanwhile, Marlene, to whom I had earlier sent the image, commented by phone that it was a "nice pic." By then, the original stack of stones and my photograph of it no longer existed.

And I thought of those far away bright stars still observable in the night sky, some of which have already exploded and no longer exist —and we just don't know it yet.

Sirens and Muses

Along the shoals,
with irresistible calls
and promises of pleasure or safety,
the temptress lures
the offshore sailors
who struggle in the foamy waves.

The witless sailors, entranced and confused,
unmoored from their old yearnings of home
feel only the inviting landward pull
of the sirens.

No longer heeding the voices of reason
or the inner compass
that reads to them the consequences
of their actions,
they turn their ships to land
and the fates that await them
in the foamy lather of sea waves
dashing on the slicing rocks
that splinter the water-logged ships
and toss the crew to their seaward grave.

The muse does not call
so insistently from afar;
she waits quietly, but willingly,
from within for the mind to be calm and still.
Like the magma working its way
through open fissures to the surface,
the words and ideas rise
as if beckoned from another place.
There is no crashing and thrashing
in the presence of the muse;
a quiet focus is required or
the inchoate ideas dissolve in the ether.

Like the oracle at Delphi
she may coax out the language in riddles
rather than insights
so even the writer on the shore of ideas
becomes the observing participant
in the co-creation of meaning
while watching them take shape before one's
own open eyes.

A Time for Letting Go

In the letting go
        so much is possible

unwinding the tightened grip,
the holding on of pain

conforming to a way

the giant oak in autumn
        without clinging
        releases its golden leaves

the sequoia
        its needles
                fall through misty fog

a soaring eagle
        surrenders to warm air current and updraft
                effortless
                floating
                across valleys

a last breath
deferred for a lifetime
        waiting for acceptance
                deciding alone
                that it is time

Letting go seeks no reward
        no continuation
                of what once was;
the leaves and needles,
        feathers and pain,
                removed from the cycle
                of returning

Others come along
        appearing first as
        separate leaves and dewdrops
        before coming to understand
        it is one forest, one ocean

In the letting go of effort
        and strivings
        and enduring self

what awaits behind the letting go
        is known only by
                the having done it.

In the Cave of Habit

In this version of the story of Plato's Cave, I am seated in the front row. I have come to learn this from someone seated to my immediate right. This person sits at the end of the front row. I can see him if I strain hard enough and stretch my torso and head. I can also turn slightly to my left and glimpse several others beside me. With the shackles holding me in place, very little movement is possible, and I cannot turn to see if there are other rows behind, but the man to my right has told me that there are many others behind us. He knows this and much more because, over time and with great effort and perseverance, he has broken free of his shackles and managed to leave his place on this floor where the rest of us are seated.

He has walked up a dirt path incline leading out of this large cave and has seen a world and experienced a reality that seems, at first, too fantastic to be believed, but he returns each time to tell me of a world beyond this cave that is as seductive as it is beautiful in the way he describes it. He says that by going outside of this reality to which I and the others have grown accustomed and habituated, he better understands our reality than he would if he had remained here all his life.

He has told me that when he first broke free of the bindings and shackles and looked around, he discovered that our visual reality is actually a shadow show. The way he explained it is that shadows of objects are cast upon the wall in front of us, and we are mistakenly assuming that those shadows are objects in themselves, when in actuality far behind us there is a fire burning and objects are being placed in front of the firelight. It is the shadows of these objects that we take to be reality. He tells me that our view and understanding of our condition is very limited and that if we would only loosen these shackles we would see the habits of mind that limit our view of reality and the possibilities that await us if we are willing to break the bonds of habit and security to which we have become accustomed.

He sits next to me with the chains and straps loosely draped over his legs. It seems that he returns from his wanderings for my benefit. By instructing me about the conditioning that I and others around me have succumbed to, he hopes that someday I, too, will break free of the bindings that hold me in place. Much like the others seated to my left, I have been lulled into a sense of security. Not only do I not seek an existence beyond this present life of watching the show on the wall, but I have until recently been uninterested in even considering that there might be a different way of living or understanding beyond what I have been accustomed to for these many years.

Recently, when my friend returned from one of his expeditions, he told me what it was like the first time he ventured up the sloping earthen walkway and out of the cave. He described an intensity of light far brighter than the fire in the cave. It required several outings before he could walk about without shielding his eyes from the bright light of daytime wanderings. His first descriptions were difficult for me to understand because I had no experience or vocabulary for what he was describing. These descriptions provided for me the seeds of restlessness that grew into curiosity and an open willingness to examine the constraints that kept me fastened to the ground in this cave. Much time was to pass before I had my own experiences outside the cave, and this brings me to the next part of my reflections on habits of mind and their consequences.

The difficulty with language and conveying meaning to someone else was stated by Krishnamurti, who frequently said that "the description is not the described." Years later, when I was briefly introduced to semiotics, I came to understand the parallel terms of "signifier" and "signified." The object that I am seated at (the "signified") we might call "a desk," and we have adopted the linguistic convention of the word "desk" as the "signifier" when referring to this particular object. The abstract concept has come to represent the concrete physical object. So, at the moment, there is a fleeting connection of meanings that is escaping my ability to convey in words. I wish to connect my imagined experience in Plato's cave with a phrase that was used by Krishnamurti during his talks in Ojai, California, and connect that further to the observation made by Henry David Thoreau in *Walden*, where he announced that he was determined to live his life deliberately, unlike the many around him who lived their lives of quiet desperation. For two years and two months Thoreau deliberately challenged the habits of mind to discover what the world had to teach him by interacting directly with it, observing the seasons and wildlife around Walden Pond.

In the imagined story of my presence in Plato's cave, I learn from someone else that there is a world beyond the one by which I have been conditioned. Removing the straps and bindings of security and comfort, I learned to take the first tentative steps to the path that led out of the cave into a wooded place that at first seemed unfamiliar and new. But, as I came to understand it further, I had been so long estranged from this natural world that the cave of security and habit and conformity came to seem like the only acceptable or real existence. The comforts and conveniences and predictability lulled me and others into habits of thinking and living that contributed to a growing complacency. In fact, the real home was always for my ancestors of 500 generations, close to the trees, waters, and animals that shared the places from which we have continually migrated. Stepping out of the cave provided a kind of re-acquaintance with a natural world that is, itself, being transformed and threatened by modern values increasingly disconnected from the land that could be nurturing and revitalizing all of us.

A Day in Oraibi

When I was 19 years old I stopped at Oraibi, in northeast Arizona. I had been driving my red 1966 Volkswagen bug around the American Southwest and one of my destinations was the small Hopi village that is the second longest continually inhabited settlement in North America. My recollection from this distance of 50 years is that the desert in that region was flat as far as the eye could see, except for the long rocky butte or mesa that rose abruptly to a height of 200 feet, like a spine running above the dry desert floor. There was a small parking area, but this was no tourist spot, even though it appeared that people were permitted to come to this location. A permanent sign stated: No Cameras Beyond This Point.

I don't recall how I actually introduced myself to Gorman David, but soon we were talking about his home and the region. He told me that he was proud of his people and wanted me and others to know about them. Even though I imagine he said this routinely to visitors at Oraibi, I felt he was inviting me beyond the line where most visitors turned around and returned to their cars. He guided me to the top of the mesa where we looked out over the desert. He pointed out the way the rock had been scooped out to collect snow for a fresh water source, and he said his people knew where to grow corn down below on the desert floor above secret water sources. He led me into his family's small living quarters and I remember him opening a small wooden hope chest and removing a black dress made of beads or small dried beans. It was a very delicate and fragile old dress that belonged to his grandmother. As he was showing me around his personal lodging, his father arrived. Gorman David told me that his father was the Chieftain of the Snake Clan. The father and son exchanged some words in their Hopi language, and although I did not understand what they were saying, my clear sense at the time was that his father disapproved of my presence in their private dwelling. Gorman David, again, conveyed to me that he was proud of his people and, unlike his father, he wanted to share information and personal details about the Hopis.

Then Gorman David invited me to join him that evening in the kiva, where each Saturday they had a sacred ceremony. I thanked him, but declined the offer, saying that I believed his father was upset with my presence, and it seemed disrespectful that this unknown visitor would attend their sacred ceremony.

As we continued to talk outside his family home atop the butte, a younger and shorter Indian approached. As they were exchanging a few words, the young man began reaching his arm into the inside sleeve of Gorman David's jacket, struggling to retrieve what turned out to be a half-pint of brandy that Gorman David had concealed in his jacket sleeve the entire time I had been there. The young man unscrewed the cap, took a quick swig and finished off the bottle, then threw it out over the abutment into the sandy desert far below. In a matter of minutes I had gone from the possibility of accepting an invitation to witness a sacred Hopi ceremony to a disillusionment that complicated my understanding of what the Hopi people were experiencing at this point in their history. This also hastened my departure.

I don't recall if Gorman David told me—or I heard it later—that alcohol was destroying the Hopis and the nearby Navajos. It seemed evident from my brief visit that a younger generation was indeed being lured away from the sacred tradition and history of the people that had survived for a hundred generations in this region.

As I prepared to leave and said goodbye to Gorman David, he said that someday I will come back. He wanted to leave me with some certainty of this, so he said before nightfall it will rain hard. With the hot summer day and blue sky as far as I could see, I felt that the alcohol had influenced his sense of pride and common sense. So, I made my way down to the car and drove off, replaying the scenes and feelings I had experienced that afternoon in Oraibi. In the hours before nightfall, the sky darkened and the rain did fall, a heavy downpour that has stayed with me for these 50 years. There is still a pull toward Oraibi, and the possibility remains that I will return someday.

Colonized in Paradise

I was taking my tourist photographs
of the early morning Waikiki shoreline,
unselfconsciously wearing my December white legs in public.
In spare time, reading Davenport, Tyau, and Trask,
feeling forever the outsider among the Disneyized hotel guests,
feeling like part of the invasion that has taken this beautiful island
from its people.

I want only this warm sun, this warm sand—not the history
that has brought me here.

In that morning when only a few early risers were strolling
on the beach, I lowered the camera for a woman to pass.
She sat on the short wall, removed her flip-flops and muumuu,
        and rested in her one-piece bathing suit,
        dangling her legs and facing the early morning sun.
        Maybe age 60, I guess, with weathered face
        and tanned arms and legs, pleasant person.

I asked something about the swimming and she said
this was her day off. She usually comes here at 5:00 in the morning
to swim in the ocean for 10 minutes before going to work
in one of the hotels. I imagined her head bobbing in the darkness,
buoyant in the calm early morning sea, splashing warm water over
her face while the tourists slept, enjoying a moment of undisturbed
peace in this paradise before subjecting herself to the invisibility she
would face in her day among expectant guests. She said the water is
very refreshing, her soft Filipino voice filled with kindness.

Why does this brief encounter, a few words on the beach
with the woman whose name I'll never know,
mean more to me than all the people around the pool
and in the Jacuzzi from all the states of the union?
Why do I feel that this is a continuation of the brutality
that began here generations ago?

This woman is transplanted, not a native. Even the women in the
convenience store who played the CD about Hawaiians crying for
the loss of Hawaii were not from here. It's like Baudrillard's
hyperreal description of young Hispanic girls working the cash
registers in the gift shop at the Alamo.

The commodification of the colonized. Where are the tracings
and fingerprints of the history that led to this?
The air and music are filled with reminders that the people here
were robbed, but the blood has been washed away
and new hotels have sprouted overtop an earlier culture.

The luau was a painful remake of the black-face vaudeville shows.
Native residents uncomfortably dressed in "traditional" costumes,
getting the audience to laugh at the fact that the coconuts
in the display come from Walmart. A commentary on the loss of
culture becomes camp and a source of self-deprecating humor.
The audience drinks more rum and laughs it away. This is paradise
and they are on vacation. I am on vacation too. Am I one of them?

A week later, while snorkeling in Kapalua, Maui, I see the fish that
swim in schools beneath the surface of things, getting what they need
from what is tossed up by the currents. The Filipino woman, far
away in Waikiki, swam again this morning at 5:00 before going to
work in the hotels.

Cultivating Serendipity

Today at Balboa Park in San Diego we walked through an outdoor open space where artists were exhibiting and selling their creations. I passed booths displaying paintings and one that had large flower vases with abstract colorful designs that lead me to consider asking a question about the process of creating such art. I didn't ask the woman who was apparently the artist, but continued walking, trying to formulate the question.

At a nearby booth an older man was standing next to his glazed pottery that included dishes, clay vases, and other utilitarian objects. I said to him, "This is a question that I could ask any artist, but when you start working on something, how close is the finished result to what you set out to create?" It wasn't quite phrased the way I would have liked, but he was polite and kind in responding: "It's always very much like what I set out to create. Any artist has to know what they want the result to look like."

He pointed to a stack of four blue and white glazed bowls with gently swirling shapes that made them look similar, but not identical. I followed up: "Is there any place for serendipity in your work?" He said, "Yes, when I place these objects in the kiln, I don't always know what will result from the thickness of the glaze or the variations in temperature." Then he said something that has stayed with me ever since: "I plan for serendipity."

He has been working with his craft for 50 years, and it was evident from his expertise that he could control much of the outcome in his work. He said at times something magical happens and pointed to a large object on display in the nearby gift shop. He asked me to go look at it, reminding me, as we parted, that everything operates within the laws of physics. But at times, he said, it is a wonder how the effect is achieved. I walked into the gift store and the object to which he was referring seemed as if it would topple because of the unequal weight distribution. But this experienced potter had found a way to create something beyond what most artists achieve.

Another point he made, with some pride, is that the bottom of his pottery was glazed; he said this sets his work apart from others, explaining that the pottery has to rest on the bottom in the kiln, but he found a way to glaze the bottom so that it doesn't scratch any surface that the object rests on. The magical and the role of serendipity. This brought to mind something I had witnessed five months earlier.

At Indian Cave, near Shubert, Nebraska, the small wooden C. McDowell Bridge leads across a creek to the Living History Log Cabin, where a small group of people, consisting mostly of volunteers, shows passersby the crafts of making lye soap (to treat poison ivy and poison oak) and working with metals. The blacksmith was an old timer who enjoyed discussing the details of his craft, including the temperatures of the heated metals he worked with.

He had recently purchased the last ton of coal he may be able to obtain for some time that produces the high temperatures that he requires in forging his metal implements. In the midst of his discussion he introduced the idea of "magic" that occurs in his craft after many years of experience. Specifically, he was referring to a challenge that he undertook to encase a small glass marble in a handle he had crafted from three entwining lengths of metal. The challenge, he pointed out, was that a glass marble will crack or explode at temperatures (1600 degrees Fahrenheit) lower than what is needed to bend the metal rods (2200 degrees Fahrenheit) he was twining around the marble. He discovered that as the metal cools there is a moment —only a few seconds long—when he is able to continue twisting the metal tighter around the glass marble. He described it as magical when it happens. He showed me the end product of a glass agate contained within three evenly spaced twisted metal strands fashioned into a teardrop shape that served as the handle for a fireplace poker. The effect was beautiful and mysterious.

Two artists, potter and blacksmith, working with different media, each experiencing after decades of perfecting his craft, those moments of magical and serendipitous transformation and insight. Each pushing his art into the new and unexpected territory of his craft. It isn't that they are counting on chance to bring about something wonderful, but instead honing their craft so that there is room for those uncontrolled elements—whether it's the cooling metal surrounding a fragile glass marble or the way the glaze spreads over pottery in the kiln—to work for them in creating something beautiful, mysterious, and maybe even inexplicable. Serendipity—not controlled or manipulated—but incorporated into the art where room is made available for those chance occurrences.

In the Light of the Full Moon (Reprise)

At the edge of thought
      looking over the abyss
      lunacy awaits

like laughter carried in the wind
      taunting one to leap
      into the belief that one can fly
      and glide from world to world
      as if the universe is keeping tally
      of good and bad deeds

and the words uttered at the time of death
      carry more meaning
      than a lifetime of word cargo—
      purchased like a train ticket into another existence.

I stand at the edge, staring into the maw of lunacy,
      feet firmly grounded, and down below
      the carcasses and dried bones
      of buffalo and people
      who thought they could fly
      into some next world,

and I wonder, with awe, at the beauty in this life
      that they all traded for the hope
      of something better beyond this wondrous place.

I will stay here and cultivate
      the seeds of reason
      and water them with practice and study,
      learning that what I see and experience
      doesn't require leaping over the edge
      into belief and faith and hope,
      for it is lunacy to be drawn over the edge
      by the moon's promise of a better existence than this.

Descending

In my distant ancestors
    the larynx had not yet descended,
    leaving them uttering with guttural sounds
    and bilabial plosives;
    some of them added clicking sounds
    to their repertoire of vocalizations.

This was before they learned to carry fire
    in their mushroom-toting pouches;
    and the only cooked meat
    came from lightning strikes.

They were keen hunters
    with a sense of sound and smell
    that we have lost during these 10,000 generations.

Now, with intact voice box
    we search for someone to talk to;
    our modern tribe carries little machines that do the talking,
    and our opposable thumbs have grown arthritic
    from tapping on screens.

Each new generation brings its own distractions
    and a million conveniences before imponderable death.

Some will bury their dead;
    some will travel to distant planets;
    some will wake from dreams
    and share them with others under the stars.

Resuming the Search

We searched the archives
>to see if we had been here before
>maybe some stone carvings would provide a clue
>or maybe a clay mask would fit my face perfectly.

Perhaps some petroglyphs would indicate a neighboring
>clan that we could recognize as an old neighbor
>or we might find a burial shroud
>with the imprint of your deep eye sockets
>>and high cheekbones.

We sought some recognizable shard or urn
>we used for storing freshly pressed oil
>when we inhabited the fertile desert.

Going further back we searched the rocky mountainside
>for fossils of our fish forebears
>and we looked in the tar pits
>to see if we may have been trapped and preserved by surprise.

We excavated the depths of volcanic ash
>for a hint of how we once lived in community

and we studied the fossilized leaves that would have been our food
>when we lived among the treetops.

We collected and filed the tracings
>of where we likely swam and roamed long ago
>in so many places we called home

and now we sift again among the collections we gathered,
>mapping out the most likely course that led us here,
>trying to retrace our steps
>to see if all those clues
>might tell us where we're going.

Future in the Present

To test whether there is a future
        we visualized a time when we would travel
        to the blue zones
        and we saw health and warm sand
        in the wispy salt air;

        we imagined cool afternoon breezes
            accompanying the fragrant taste
            of papaya and bananas;

        soon we saw ourselves planning,
        bringing our present toward the future,
        remembering that this, too, would be impermanent—
        as we flowed in a current that we were not controlling.

And we reached the sandy coast and the sun—
        as warm and comforting as we could ever imagine—
        and in the knowing that these days too would end,
        we did not prolong or attempt to repeat those moments,
        but with gratitude we looked on,
            glimpsing equanimity in the moving present
            like the movement of breaking waves
            in the ocean's stillness.

Meeting the Deep Past in Burro Creek

I stand
as representative
of earth's self-reflecting consciousness
in the desert of the American Southwest

Full moon rising over morning canyon
reflecting the sun's light faintly
against the layered canyon walls
—a message of earth's aging contained at a fault line
        of tectonic subduction

I stare at one speckled granite rock before me
itself containing all that I need to know
but do not understand

Among the boulders in the upthrust
this one is rounded smooth
with two deep holes like eye sockets
burrowed, one might guess,
by the slow and constant dripping of water
for a duration far beyond human time

Before speaking, I run my fingers into
the deep circular tubes
worn smooth in hardest rock
by the dripping of soft silky water

"Dear modest old rock, resting here for a time,
        wearing down so slowly that
        all of humanity could walk by
        and say good morning—
        I have come here to learn patience and perseverance."

About the Author

Don Langford was born in Ontario, Canada, and grew up in Southern California. He received his BA in English from Oregon State University where he was the recipient of an Academy of American Poets Award and the winner of the first Roger Weaver Poetry Prize at Oregon State. He earned a doctorate in English from The Ohio State University after completing his dissertation entitled *The Primacy of Place in Gary Snyder's Ecological Vision*. His poem "Vivid Dreams, Antarctica" was nominated for a Pushcart Prize and he has published poems in several literary magazines. After teaching for more than 25 years in the English Department at The Ohio State University, he now devotes his time to writing poetry and traveling full-time with his wife, Marlene, in their RV.